My Weird Sc... FAST FACTS

Mummies, Myths, and Mysteries

Also by Dan Gutman

My Weird School

My Weird School Daze

My Weirder School

My Weirdest School

My Weirder-est School

My Weird School Fast Facts

The Baseball Card Adventure series

The Genius Files

The Flashback Four series

Rappy the Raptor

Johnny Hangtime

My Weird School
FAST FACTS
Mummies, Myths, and Mysteries

Dan Gutman

Pictures by
Jim Paillot

HARPER
An Imprint of HarperCollinsPublishers

To Nina

The author gratefully acknowledges the editorial contributions of Nina Wallace.

Photograph credits: Page 8: Jason Benz Bennee / Shutterstock; Page 16: Pius Lee / Shutterstock; Page 31: Kokhanchikov / Shutterstock; Page 38: Sean M Smith / Shutterstock; Page 45: Ewa Studio / Shutterstock; Page 50: AndreyO / Shutterstock; Page 57: Janusz Pienkowski / Shutterstock; Page 64: Courtesy of the Library of Congress; Page 75: Mati Nitibhon / Shutterstock; Page 78: mtkang / Shutterstock; Page 80: giannimarchetti / Shutterstock; Page 108: Cris Foto / Shutterstock; Page 110: Courtesy of the Walters Art Museum; Page 118: Viacheslav Lopatin / Shutterstock; Page 121: Nenad Basic / Shutterstock; Page 122: Claudio Divizia / Shutterstock; Page 125: Belenos / Shutterstock; Page 132: Luxerendering / Shutterstock; Page 143: Roberta Canu / Shutterstock; Page 166: Alessandro DYD / Shutterstock; Page 169: Dave Head / Shutterstock; Page 176: Courtesy of the Library of Congresss

My Weird School Fast Facts: Mummies, Myths, and Mysteries
Text copyright © 2019 by Dan Gutman
Illustrations copyright © 2019 by Jim Paillot

ISBN 978-0-06-267312-1 (pbk. bdg.) — ISBN 978-0-06-267313-8 (library bdg.)

Typography by Laura Mock
19 20 21 22 23   PC/BRR   10 9 8 7 6 5 4 3 2 1
❖
First Edition

Contents

The Beginning

 Howdy, fellow weirdos! This is your old pal, Professor A.J. Did you know the ancient Egyptians invented toothpaste? It's true! I'm in the gifted and talented program at school, so I know lots of stuff that normal kids don't know. So nah-nah-nah boo-boo on you!

Okay, you want to know a secret?

Ancient history is a super snooze. Who cares about stuff that happened thousands of years ago? Not me. I don't even care what happened last week.

 Now wait one gosh-darned minute there, Arlo!

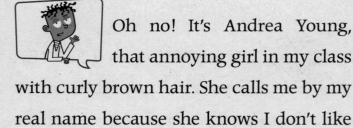 Oh no! It's Andrea Young, that annoying girl in my class with curly brown hair. She calls me by my real name because she knows I don't like it. Who invited Little Miss Know-It-All?*

 You know perfectly well that we're supposed to work on

---

* Andrea is a poopyhead.

this project *together*, Arlo. And ancient history is *fascinating*. I bet most kids don't know that the ancient Egyptians liked bowling. I bet most kids don't know that the ancient Greeks figured out the size of the earth, and that the sun is the center of the solar system. I bet most kids don't know that people in ancient Rome ate stork, roast parrot, flamingo, and peacock tongues.

 And I bet most kids don't know that the ancient Egyptians used to pull the brains out of mummies through their noses.

We're not going to talk about gross stuff here, Arlo!

Remember we talked about that? No disgusting things. And no toilet stuff.

 Okay, okay! You're no fun at all.

 Writing this book is going to be *lots* of fun, Arlo! We're going to tell the readers all kinds of cool stuff, like how ancient people lived, what they wore, what they ate, what they believed, and what they did for fun.

 I can tell the readers one thing right now. Ancient people were weird.

Yours truly,

Professor A.J.

(the professor of awesomeness)

 Andrea Young (future Harvard graduate)*

---

* Arlo is *so* immature.

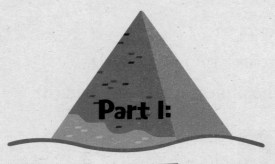

Part I:

Ancient Egypt

 Ancient Egypt was one of the greatest and most powerful civilizations in history. It was rich in culture, government, religion, and the arts. It lasted for over three *thousand* years. The United States of America isn't even three *hundred* years old.

ZZZZZ. Oh, sorry, I must have dozed off there for a minute.

Were you talking about how the Egyptians pulled the brains of mummies out through their noses?

No! Nobody cares about that stuff, Arlo. If we're going to talk about ancient Egypt, we should start by talking about *important* things, like . . .

The Pyramids

I think the coolest thing about ancient Egypt was the pyramids. Just look at them! They were built thousands of years ago, and they're still there! My grandpa's house was built less than a hundred years ago, and last year they tore it down and replaced it with a parking lot.

 Arlo and I had lots of questions about the pyramids. We had to do a lot of research to answer them. . . .

How big are the pyramids?

 The largest one is the Great Pyramid of Giza. It's over 480

feet tall. That's taller than the Statue of Liberty. It weighs as much as sixteen Empire State Buildings. For almost four thousand years, it was the tallest man-made structure in the world.

Are all pyramids the same?

No. There are around eighty pyramids that are still in Egypt, and they're different sizes and shapes. The first pyramids were called "step pyramids," because they have ledges that look like big steps. The earliest one that still exists today was built in 2630 BCE. As their technology advanced, the Egyptians built bigger pyramids with smoother, sloping sides.

Why were the pyramids built?

They were built as burial places for the pharaohs—the leaders of the Egyptian empire. The Great Pyramid of Giza was built for King Khufu.

What's inside the pyramids?

There was the burial chamber for the pharaoh, of course. There were also burial chambers for his family and his servants. The walls are often covered with carvings and paintings. Some of the pyramids have lots of rooms and passageways. Some rooms were filled with the pharaoh's treasures and personal belongings.

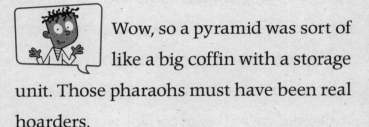 Wow, so a pyramid was sort of like a big coffin with a storage unit. Those pharaohs must have been real hoarders.

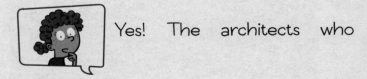 Actually, they were buried with their belongings because it was believed the pharaoh would need all that stuff after he died.

Did people try to steal all that stuff?

Yes! The architects who

11

designed the pyramids tried to fool grave robbers by putting in fake entrances, false doors, and passages that led to empty rooms. They used heavy granite doors that were almost impossible to move. But the thieves were smart, and over the centuries nearly all the pyramids were broken into. Many treasures were stolen.

Who built the pyramids?

It took around ten thousand workers more than thirty years to build a pyramid. For a long time, experts believed that slaves were forced to build them. Now we know that the pyramid builders had hard lives, but they did get paid for their work. They must have been respected too, because the ones who died during construction were buried in tombs near the pyramids of their pharaohs.

How were the pyramids built?

It wasn't easy! First, the workers cut large blocks of

limestone. Then they pulled the blocks up the pyramid with ropes, using wooden sleds on top of round logs. To this day, we marvel at how much the Egyptians were able to accomplish without trucks, cranes, or any of the other heavy machinery we use to build things today.

It took so long to build a pyramid that the pharaohs would usually start building one as soon as they became ruler. That way, it would be ready by the time they died.

When did they stop building pyramids?

 Around 2150 BCE, the age of the pyramids came to an end.

After that, most of the pharaohs were buried in a part of Egypt called the Valley of the Kings, which was west of the Nile River. The tombs could be hidden high in the cliffs there, and the valley had a narrow entrance that could be guarded. Maybe that's why grave robbers never broke into the tomb of King Tut. We'll talk more about him later.

What's with that weird statue near the Great Pyramid of Giza?

 That's the Sphinx.

 The *what*?

The Sphinx.

That word definitely looks like it's spelled wrong.

It's not. A sphinx is an imaginary creature that has the body of a lion and the head of a person—often a pharaoh or a god. There are lots of them in Egypt. They were built to guard tombs and temples.

I guess they didn't do a very good job, then. Maybe if the Egyptians had hired *human* guards, the grave robbers wouldn't have stolen all that stuff from the tombs.

Here's a weird fast fact about the Sphinx at Giza—it has no nose. Somewhere down the line, the nose got knocked off. Some people say Turkish soldiers who were taking target practice shot it off. Other people say it was chiseled off by somebody who thought it was evil. We'll never know for sure. It's one of those ancient mysteries.

Mummies

 Speaking of ancient myster-
ies, mummies are really
mysterious.

 They're cool too. Gross, but
cool. I'm not sure if I men-
tioned this earlier, but they used to pull
out the brains of mummies through their
noses.

 You *did* mention it, Arlo. But
we should probably start by
telling the readers that the ancient Egyptians believed that after a person died, he

or she would pass into an afterlife. It was supposed to be a lot like real life, so the body would need to be preserved as long as possible. The process of preserving the body was called "embalming," and the embalmed body was a mummy.

I know everything there is to know about embalming and mummies. First, priests would wash the body. If you're going to eternity you want to be clean, right?* Then they would pull out all of the dead person's organs. That must have been weird to

* This is when stuff starts getting gross. If you like gross stuff, you're in luck!

take an organ out of a body. Why would there be musical instruments inside a body anyway?

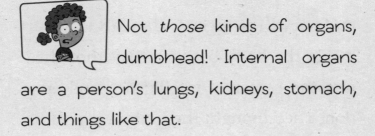 Not *those* kinds of organs, dumbhead! Internal organs are a person's lungs, kidneys, stomach, and things like that.

 I knew that. I was just yanking your brain. Anyway, they would use a long stick that got inserted into the nostrils to dig out the brain. Then they would roll the body over so the liquid would drain through the nose hole. It was a no-brainer!

 Gross!

 I know, right? But they didn't

pull out *all* the organs. They left the heart inside the body because they thought it was the center of intelligence and emotion. They thought the brain was useless.

 Sort of like *your* brain, Arlo!

 Funny. So funny that I forgot to laugh.

 What did they do with all those organs they took out?

 They put them into containers called "canopic jars" and

left them in the burial tomb with the body. They would have four canopic jars—one for the stomach, one for the intestines, one for the lungs, and one for the liver. Next, they would carefully label the jars and put them in the refrigerator so people wouldn't confuse them with last night's leftovers.

Arlo, that's ridiculous! They didn't have refrigerators in ancient Egypt!

 I know that. I just wanted to see if you were paying attention. It would be weird to take some leftover spaghetti out of your refrigerator and then find out it was some dead guy's intestines.

Anyway, next they would fill the body with sawdust or linen stuffing to make it look the way the person looked before their insides were removed. After that, the body would be covered with stuff called "natron," which was like salt. It drew moisture out. Then they would let the body dry for around forty days.

Wow, I had no idea this was such a complicated process!

Oh yeah. It could take months to finish making a mummy. After the body was dry, oils would be rubbed on the skin to preserve it, and the mummy would be wrapped in linen from head to toe. If you unwrapped all the bandages of an Egyptian mummy and put them together, they would stretch for nearly a mile. Glue was used to hold the layers together. Finally, a shroud was put over the mummy, and then the mummy would be placed in a stone or wooden coffin called a "sarcophagus."

 Many mummies have been lost to history. Some of them were burned for fuel. Some were destroyed by treasure hunters. And some were ground up into powder to make magic potions. Yuck!

 Sometimes, a mummy's mouth would be left open, so it could breathe in the afterlife.

You know, it used to be that scientists had to unwrap a mummy to examine it and learn all this stuff. But these days, they can use X-rays, MRIs, and CAT scans.

And by the way, ancient Egyptians didn't turn *every* dead person into a mummy. It was expensive, so only rich and power-ful people got the full mummy treatment.

Most Egyptians were just buried in pits in the desert.

And that's everything you need to know about mummies!

 Well, I must say, Arlo, I am impressed! You may not know anything about reading, writing, social studies, or math, but you sure know your mummies.

 Mummies are my specialty. Well, that and anything to do with ancient toilets.

 No toilet stuff!

 Okay, okay!

Egyptian Inventions

 The Egyptians invented lots of stuff we use today, like toothpaste and breath mints.

 Arlo, that's crazy!

 No, it's true! They made toothpaste out of powdered ox hooves, ashes, burnt eggshells, and pumice. I'm glad I didn't have to brush my teeth with *that* stuff. No wonder the Egyptians needed breath mints! They made them out of frankincense, myrrh, cinnamon, and honey. It was all shaped into little pellets.

 Here's something you probably don't know—the Egyptians invented eye makeup!

 No way!

 Yes way! They combined soot with a lead mineral called "galena" to create a black ointment called "kohl." Women *and* men wore eye makeup. But they didn't do it to look good. They did it because they thought makeup had healing powers.

But we should talk about the more important things the Egyptians invented. Like writing! Hieroglyphics was a form of writing using pictures. They had more than seven hundred different pictures.

Hieroglyphic drawings and paintings on the ceiling and walls of the ancient Egyptian temple of Dendera

The thing is, for almost two thousand years, nobody was able to figure out what those pictures meant. Then, in 1799, a Frenchman named Jean-François Champollion finally cracked the code by examining a piece of black stone that was found in the city of Rosetta. It had three kinds of writing on it, and one of them was Greek. Champollion could read Greek, so he was able to figure out what the hiero-glyphics meant.

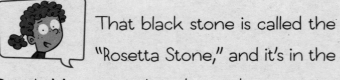

That black stone is called the "Rosetta Stone," and it's in the British Museum in London today.

A lot of Egyptian writing was found on stone tablets or walls, but they also invented a kind of paper called "papyrus." It was made from a tall reedlike plant. For over three thousand years, papyrus was state-of-the-art writing material.

 They also undertook the first major irrigation project. They built canals and ditches to get water from the Nile River and move it to faraway fields to grow crops.

 They also invented the solar calendar. The Egyptian calendar was a lot like ours. One year had 365 days and twelve months with thirty days in each month, plus an extra month of five days.

 They also invented the clock! In fact, they invented two different kinds of clocks. A "shadow clock" was sort of like a sundial. The position of the shadow that was cast would tell people what time it was. A "water clock" was made from a stone vessel that had a hole at the bottom. As the water dripped out slowly, they could tell how much time had passed. Smart!

Gods and Pharaohs

The Egyptians worshipped lots of gods—over two thousand of them! Ra was the sun god. Horus was the god of the sky. Thoth was the god of knowledge. Apophis was the god of snakes. Babi was the god of baboons. Yes, you read that right. There was a god of baboons!

The pharaoh was the leader of Egypt, and people thought of him as both a man *and* a god. In all, there were about 170 pharaohs. We don't have room to talk about all of them, but we've got to tell you about the big one. . . .

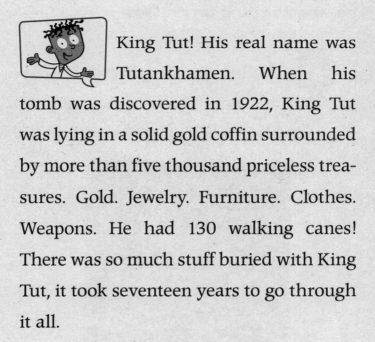 King Tut! His real name was Tutankhamen. When his tomb was discovered in 1922, King Tut was lying in a solid gold coffin surrounded by more than five thousand priceless treasures. Gold. Jewelry. Furniture. Clothes. Weapons. He had 130 walking canes! There was so much stuff buried with King Tut, it took seventeen years to go through it all.

 One of the treasures buried in King Tut's tomb was a pair

of sandals with pictures of his enemies on the soles. That way, wherever Tut went, he was stomping on his foes.

King Tut is called "The Boy King" because he became pharaoh when he was just nine years old.

King Tutankhamen's funerary mask

Can you imagine being named ruler of a country as a kid? That must have been cool. If that was me, I would have made homework illegal.

On the other hand, maybe it wasn't so great to be a kid king, because Tut died when he was eighteen years old.

Nobody knows for sure how he died. That's another ancient mystery. For a long time, archaeologists believed King Tut was murdered. There was a large hole in the back of his skull. But now they think the hole was caused by the mummification process. These days, most experts believe King

Tut died from a wound to his leg. He also suffered from malaria, and that might have killed him.

 There have even been archaeologists who believe that King Tut died from the bite of an angry hippopotamus!

 Only men were supposed to be pharaohs. Not fair! But there were some exceptions. Hatshepsut was the first female to rule with the full powers of a pharaoh. Archaeologists believe she had a skin disorder and she died after rubbing on a medicine that turned out to be poisonous. Then there was Queen Nefertiti. She's often called "the most beautiful woman in the world." And finally, of course, there was the last pharaoh of Egypt—Cleopatra.

 She has an amazing story. Listen to this. When Cleopatra was eighteen years old, her father died. She and her brother Ptolemy XIII became co-pharaohs. But he was just ten, so Cleopatra was in charge. As Ptolemy got older, he decided to take control. He kicked Cleopatra out of the palace and took over as pharaoh.

Well, she didn't like that, so she built an army and formed

an alliance with the Roman emperor Julius Caesar. We'll talk more about him in Part 3. They also happened to fall in love.

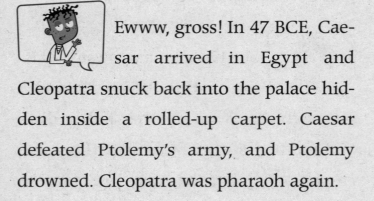 Ewww, gross! In 47 BCE, Caesar arrived in Egypt and Cleopatra snuck back into the palace hidden inside a rolled-up carpet. Caesar defeated Ptolemy's army, and Ptolemy drowned. Cleopatra was pharaoh again.

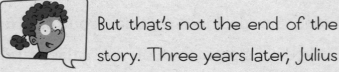 But that's not the end of the story. Three years later, Julius Caesar was assassinated. His son Octavian became the leader of the Roman Empire. A Roman general named Mark Antony

wasn't happy about that, so he teamed up with Cleopatra to go to war with Octavian. They also fell in love.

Ewww, gross!

Sadly, Cleopatra and Marc Antony lost the war and died by suicide in 30 BCE. Cleopatra let herself be bitten by a poisonous snake called an "asp." The ending to the story is that Octavian took control of Egypt and it became part of the Roman Empire. And that was the end of the ancient Egyptian Empire.

More Weird Fast Facts about Ancient Egypt . . .

 Some experts believe the first pharaoh was named Aha. Aha!

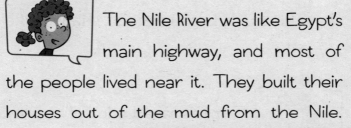 The Nile River was like Egypt's main highway, and most of the people lived near it. They built their houses out of the mud from the Nile.

 The river also provided food, soil, water, and transportation. Most of the country was desert, but the land near the Nile was good for growing barley, flax, and wheat.

According to the ancient Egyptians, the earth was flat and round like a pancake. What were they thinking? Now, of course, we know that the earth is square and shaped like a waffle.

Families saved a lot of money on clothing, because kids under the age of six often didn't wear any clothes at all.

Boys under twelve years old had their heads shaved except for one braided lock. This was supposed to protect them from lice and fleas.

While ancient Egyptians made many advancements that we still use, they practiced some cures for ailments and diseases that we would never try today. Believing it would cure blindness, they would mash up a pig's eye, mix it with red ochre (a kind of iron ore), and pour it into the person's ear!

 Do you know how they treated infections? They put moldy bread on them.

 One cure for bed-wetting was to tie a bag full of mouse bones around the person's neck before they went to sleep at night. You should try that, Arlo.

 Your *face* looks like a bag of mouse bones!

The Egyptians thought cats brought good luck, and considered them to be sacred. When a cat died, the owners would mourn by shaving off their eyebrows. Their *own* eyebrows. They also liked dogs, lions, and baboons. Ancient tombs contained lots of mummies of people's pets.

Pharaoh Pepi II came up with an idea to keep flies off him. He would order some naked slaves to stand near him and have honey smeared all over them. So the flies would bother the slaves instead of him. While that sounds awful to us today, you have to remember that pharaohs had almost unlimited power.

The ancient Egyptians mostly used donkeys as their beasts of burden. It wasn't until much later that they used camels.

 They judged a man's status by the length of his beard, and they would wear fake beards. Regular people wore small beards about two inches long. Kings wore longer beards with square ends. The gods had the longest beards, and these were curled up at the tip.

Illustration of the Egyptian god Osiris, depicting a curled beard

Because they consumed so much beer, wine, bread, and

honey, the Egyptian pharaohs were often overweight.

 They should have gone on Weight Watchers. It worked for my mom.

 Guess what Egyptian pillows were made out of.

 Discarded mummy brains?

 No, rocks!

 Ouch! That's gotta hurt. Hey,

did you know that Egyptian police offi-
cers out on patrol would sometimes have
monkey assistants?

I did. Did you know that kids
liked to play with spinning
tops, clay balls, and wooden animals? They
also played leapfrog, jacks, and tug-of-
war. And get this—the Egyptians liked
bowling! In the town of Narmoutheos,
archaeologists found a room with a bunch
of lanes and balls.

A lot of ancient tombs had
toilets in them. But sadly,
magazines hadn't been invented yet, so

constipated Egyptians had nothing to do while they were sitting on the bowl.

 No toilet stuff, Arlo! Let's move on to our next ancient civilization.

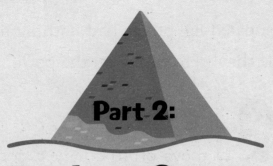

Part 2:

Ancient Greece

Greece was a world super-power almost four thousand years ago. The Greeks created the foundations of modern civilization, developing new ideas for government, science, art, literature, architecture, theater, and sports. Lots of these ideas are still with us today.

I saw *Grease* once. It was cool. They had a car right on the stage.

 Not *Grease*, Arlo! Greece!

 I knew that. I was just yanking your chain, Andrea. I know the Greeks invented all kinds of cool stuff. Did you know they invented birthday candles? It's true! It all began when people brought cakes with candles on them to the temple of Artemis, the goddess of the hunt.

 Are you making that up, Arlo?

 No! The Greeks also invented the first vending machine. People would drop a coin in, and holy water would come out.

 Really?

 Yup, and get this. Are you sitting down? This is the most amazing thing of all. The Greeks invented socks! Yes, socks! Around 700 BCE, some guy named Hesiod wrote poems about

what it was like to be a shepherd. In one of them, he suggested wearing sandals and a cloth made of wool or animal hair.

Portrait of Hesiod on a 50-drachma banknote, 1939 Greece

 That's very interesting. But I think we should talk about the more *important* innovations that came from ancient Greece.

I think socks are pretty important.

Great Greek Innovations

How about democracy? *That's* pretty important. In the sixth century BCE, the Greeks developed a new system of government. Every citizen had the right to vote and participate in politics. In fact, the word "idiot" in

Greek meant a person who didn't participate in politics. And the word "democracy" comes from the Greek word "demokratia," which means "the rule of the people."

A poet named Solon was elected ruler of Athens in 594 BCE. He usually gets credit for planting the seeds of democracy. He also freed Athenian citizens who'd been enslaved because they couldn't pay their debts and made it illegal for any Athenian to be a slave.

The Greeks invented the Olympics too. They loved sports. Kids played all kinds of games.

They juggled. They played a piggyback game called "ephedrismos." They played a game like jacks using the knucklebones of sheep or goats. They played passe-boule, in which you tried to throw a ball through a hole in a board, sort of like basketball. For a ball, they used a pig bladder!

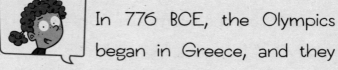 In 776 BCE, the Olympics began in Greece, and they were held every four years for the next thousand years. Athletes from city-states all over Greece came to compete. If two city-states were at war, they would have a cease-fire during the Olympics.

Women weren't allowed to compete in the Olympics. No fair! They weren't even allowed to attend! That's because the athletes competed without any clothes on.

 What?! They'd run around naked?

 Yup. In fact, the word "gym-

nasium" comes from the Greek word "gymnòs." It means "naked."

 Before a competition, the athletes would cover themselves in olive oil. Then, at the end of the day, they would scrape off the oil and their sweat. All that goopy stuff would be collected and sold as medicine. People would rub it on their skin to relieve their aches and pains.

 Ugh. That's the most disgusting thing I've ever heard.

 That's only because you haven't read the rest of this book yet.

 The winner of each competition in the Olympics was given a crown of leaves to wear on his head.

 That's *it*? They won *leaves*? No medals? No money? No Wheaties box?

 There were no Wheaties in those days, Arlo.

 The Greeks were pioneers of architecture. Whenever you see a building with tall columns, that's based on Greek buildings. The most famous temple of ancient Greece is the Parthenon. It's on a hill called the

"Acropolis" in the city of Athens, and it was built for the goddess Athena.

 The Greeks were great artists. Or sculptors, anyway. They created thousands of statues. They also enjoyed painting, but hardly any of their paintings survived because they were made on wood panels or walls that got destroyed. The one place where Greek painting survived was on pottery and ceramics. In fact, Greek pottery artists were some of the first to sign their names to their artwork.

 The Greeks were great scientists too. They figured out the size of the earth, and that the sun was the center of the solar system. They studied light and sound. They figured out how a pulley and levers work. Many of the ancient Greek discoveries and inventions are still used today.

Hippocrates was a famous

Greek scientist. Before he came along, people thought diseases were punishment from the gods. But Hippocrates studied the human body and discovered there were scientific reasons for ailments. Even today, new doctors take the Hippocratic Oath, in which they promise to uphold certain rules of medicine.

Archimedes was a Greek mathematician and inventor who created all kinds of cool stuff. He invented the odometer, which measures distance. He came up with the idea of the planetarium. He improved the catapult. He invented a screw that would lift water and pump it out of a leaking ship. He even invented a heat ray that used mirrors to reflect light and set enemy ships on fire. Archimedes was cool.

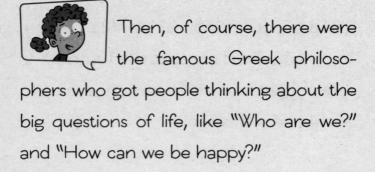 Then, of course, there were the famous Greek philosophers who got people thinking about the big questions of life, like "Who are we?" and "How can we be happy?"

 And why do farts smell?*

Not that, Arlo! Socrates was a philosopher who lived from 470 to 399 BCE. He claimed that happiness came from being a moral person rather than owning lots of stuff. His ideas

---

* Sorry, I couldn't resist. Relax! There are hardly any fart jokes in the whole book.

were so revolutionary at the time that he was considered to be a traitor. Socrates was put on trial, convicted by a jury, and sentenced to death by drinking poison. Ouch!

 Plato was a student of Socrates who tried to help people see the truth and strive to be good and fair. He believed men and women were equally intelligent, and he was one of the first to say that women

Bust of Plato in the Louvre
Paris, France

should receive the same education as men. Plato started a school called the Academy, where his students debated issues like these. The school was still going almost nine hundred years after Plato died.

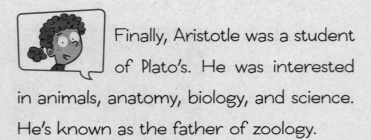 Finally, Aristotle was a student of Plato's. He was interested in animals, anatomy, biology, and science. He's known as the father of zoology.

Aristotle may have been a genius in his day, but that doesn't mean he was always right. He thought that goats could be male or female depending on which way the wind was blowing.

What?! And that guy was supposed to be a great thinker?

 Yes! The Greeks were great writers too. Homer was famous for his epic poems such as *The Iliad* and *The Odyssey*. And you've probably heard of Aesop's famous fables such as "The Boy Who Cried Wolf" and "The Tortoise and the Hare." Some phrases we still use today—"sour grapes," "crying wolf," and "lion's share"—came from Aesop's fables.

 That was long before the invention of the printing

press, of course. In those days, stories had to be carefully written down and copied by hand on scrolls. A giant library was built at Alexandria to store them all. They say it had a half a million scrolls, but we'll never know for sure. In 48 BCE, the library burned down and was lost to history for all time.

Greek writers invented three kinds of plays—comedy, tragedy, and satire. The actors wore tragic masks to show sad expressions and comic masks when their character was happy. The actors' voices would be amplified by the shape of the mask, which acted like a megaphone. Some Greek plays that were written thousands of years ago are still being performed today.

Wars and Warriors

 So we know the Greeks were great writers, artists, scientists, inventors, athletes, and philosophers. But you know what they were *really* good at?

 War?

How did you know?

It's in the heading a few lines up. There were around fifteen hundred city-states in ancient Greece, and they were constantly fighting one another. Sparta and Athens fought one war, the Peloponnesian War, for twenty-seven years. The only time the Greeks seemed to stop fighting with each other was when they were fighting against somebody *else*!

I think the most interesting war was the Trojan War in the twelfth century BCE. For ten years, Greece was at war with Troy, a Mediterranean city-state. Then, according to legend, the Greeks came up with a great idea. They built a giant horse out of wood. It was big enough so that a bunch of soldiers could hide inside it.

One night, they wheeled this "Trojan Horse" over to Troy's walls and left it there. The people of Troy thought it was a gift, and they wheeled it inside. Bad idea. In the middle of the night, Greek soldiers snuck out of the horse and took over the city. Genius!

A replica of the legendary Trojan horse used in the 2004 film *Troy*, now on display in Canakkale, Turkey

Man, those Troy dopes would fall for *anything*!

But usually, the Greeks were fighting Persia. The Persian Wars lasted over forty years, from 492 to 449 BCE. What happened was that King Darius I of Persia invaded Greece at the Bay of Marathon, which was about twenty-six miles from Athens. The Persians had more soldiers, but the Greeks were great fighters. Around six thousand Persians were killed in the battle, and then the Greek army quickly marched the twenty-six miles to Athens to protect the city. A messenger named Pheidippides ran ahead to herald the arrival of the troops. That's why today, a race of that distance is called a "marathon."

In the end, Greece won the war when Alexander the Great defeated Persia. That guy must have had a lot of confidence to call himself "the Great."

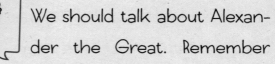 We should talk about Alexander the Great. Remember Aristotle? In 343 BCE, King Philip II of Macedonia asked him to tutor his son, Alexander. Aristotle spent years teaching the boy, who grew up to be one of the great military commanders in history.

 Alexander became the king of Greece and conquered Asia Minor, Turkey, Syria, Egypt, Babylonia, and Persia.

He never lost a battle. He was ready to conquer India when his army revolted. The soldiers wanted to go home to their families. Alexander gave in to them, but on the way home he suddenly got sick and died. He was just thirty-two. It's a mystery what he died from, but some people suspected that he was poisoned.

Ancient Roman mosaic of Alexander the Great from Pompeii, Italy

After Alexander died, the Greek empire he built was divided up between his generals. They didn't get along with each other, and gradually the empire fell apart. It was conquered by Rome in the year 146 BCE. And that was the end of the Greek empire.

Gods and Goddesses

 Arlo, do you know who was more powerful than Alexander the Great?

 Uh, Alexander the Greater?

Alexander the Greatest? Alexander the Greater-est?

 No. It was the Greek gods.

I knew that. Like the Egyptians, the ancient Greeks worshipped lots of gods and goddesses. They came from Gaea (the Earth) and Uranus (the sky). To honor the gods, temples were built in every town. Also, animals would be sacrificed to the gods—sheep, goats, pigs, cows, even fish and birds.

The king of all the gods was Zeus. He lived on Mount Olympus, a high mountain in northern Greece. Zeus could control the weather. He threw his thunderbolt like a spear.

His daughter was Athena, the goddess of wisdom. The city of Athens is named after her. Today it's the capital and the largest city in Greece.

Zeus's brother was Poseidon. He ruled the seas, and he was also the god of earthquakes and horses. Poseidon had a long beard and blue hair. He drove a golden chariot that was pulled by beasts that were half horse and half snake.

Zeus's son was Hermes. He was the messenger god, and he also invented music. The legend goes that a few minutes after he was born, Hermes picked up a tortoiseshell and tied strings across it. Then he plucked the strings to make a sound. This was the first musical instrument, called a "lyre." By the way, the word "music" comes from the Muses, goddesses of the arts.

 Ares was the god of war. He was considered to be a troublemaker, a coward, and a bully.

Aphrodite was the goddess of love. She and her son Eros would make people and gods fall in love with each other.

 Ugh! You said the L word! Disgusting!

That's silly, Arlo! Hera was the queen of the gods. She was very beautiful, and also vain about her looks. One time, she got really angry because she lost a beauty contest to Athena and Aphrodite. Another time, a queen claimed that she was more beautiful than Hera, so Hera turned the queen into a crane. That wasn't nice!

These are all ancient myths, of course. Myths are traditional stories about so-called historical events. There are lots more Greek myths and lots more gods

and goddesses to talk about, but we'll let you look them up on your own. We're not going to do *everything* for you!

More Weird Fast Facts about Ancient Greece . . .

When we have a jury trial these days, there are usually twelve people in the jury. Do you know how many people made up a jury in ancient Greece? Five hundred!

Women were considered to be second-class citizens. They weren't allowed to vote, own land, or inherit property. No fair! Men and women ate separately, and they even stayed in separate parts of a house.

The "andron" was the room

where men entertained their friends and business people.

The "gynaikon" was where women worked on weaving, spinning, and looked after their children.

Marriages in ancient Greece were arranged by the parents. Most girls got married when they were about fifteen. That may seem young, but then again, most people only lived to be thirty-five or forty.

Girls didn't have to go to school in ancient Greece. No fair! Boys shouldn't have to go to school either. But boys started school when they were seven, except in the city-state of Sparta. There, the whole educational system focused on war. Boys left home at six years old to go to military school.

Girls in Sparta also learned to be warriors and were taught how to kill. Spartans believed that strong women would make strong babies. Also, while the men were away fighting a war, the women might have to defend the city.

The Spartans were also famous for torturing prisoners, enemies, criminals, and anybody they didn't like.

 That's horrible! I don't approve of this violence.

 What do you have against violins?

 Not violins, Arlo! Violence!

 Those two words sound way too much alike, if you ask me.

 Do you know what a unibrow is? That's when somebody's eyebrows go all the way across their head with no break in the middle. In Greece, people with a unibrow were considered to be smart and beautiful. Women would even draw a line between their eyebrows to make it look like they had a unibrow.

 In ancient Greece, fat men were thought to be really good leaders.

 Do you know how the Greeks showed that they loved some-body?

 They'd throw an apple at them?

 Yes! Throwing an apple was

even used as a way to propose marriage. Would you ever throw an apple at me, Arlo?

 Maybe. But only because I want to hit you with an apple.

 Do you know how we write from left to right, and some languages are written from right to left? Well, in ancient Greece, it was common to write one line from left to right and the next line from right to left. That's weird.

 Sometimes, they would use

salt for money. That's where the phrase "not worth his salt" comes from.

 Did you know that the word "dinosaur" means "terrible lizard" in Greek?

 This is not a riddle. Why didn't they eat beans in ancient Greece?

 Is this going to be gross, Arlo?

 No! They didn't eat beans because they thought beans contained the souls of the dead.

That's interesting! And I thought you were going to say something gross.

 Who, me? Actually, in Sparta, they used to drink soup that was made from salt, vinegar, and *blood*.

 Ugh, gross! No more gross stuff, Arlo!

 Oh, then I guess you don't want to know what doctors did in ancient Greece.

 Well, that's important information. Kids need to know about that.

 Okay, you asked for it. Hip-

pocrates believed that each bodily fluid had a certain taste, and the taste would tell a doctor if something was wrong with a patient.

17th-century engraving of Hippocrates

I don't like where this is going.*

So, for example, pee was supposed to taste like fig juice. So if you went to the doctor, he would take a

* Warning! Pee and poop jokes ahead! Cover your eyes!

97

sip of your pee. If it wasn't tart enough, he
knew you had a problem.

 I'm sorry I asked.

 The doctor also might eat a
piece of your earwax, or lick
your vomit to see how sweet it was.

 I guess that's why so few
Greeks went into the field of
medicine.

 Don't you want to know how
the Greek doctors treated
scars around people's eyes?

No, I don't.

 They rubbed crocodile poop on them!

 I think I have to leave the room.

 Hey, I didn't make this stuff up. By the way, that reminds me of something. Toilet paper didn't exist in ancient Greece. Do you want to know what they used instead?

 No.

 Come on, you *know* you want to know.

 I really don't want to know, Arlo.

 I thought you wanted to know everything.

 I don't want to know *that*.

 Okay, if you insist, I'll tell you. Instead of toilet paper, the Greeks used stones!

 No way!

 Yes way! They kept a pile of rocks in their bathroom, and they had a saying: "Three stones are enough to wipe." Because, you know, they didn't want people to waste stones.

 I get it. Okay, I'm out of here. Maybe things weren't as disgusting in ancient Rome.

 Oh boy, are you in for a surprise!

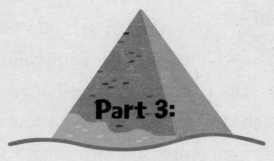

Part 3:

Ancient Rome

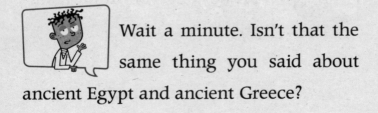

The Roman Empire was one of the greatest civilizations in the history of the world.

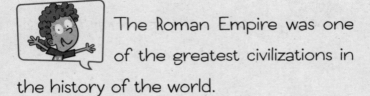

Wait a minute. Isn't that the same thing you said about ancient Egypt and ancient Greece?

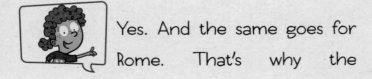

Yes. And the same goes for Rome. That's why the

Egyptians, Greeks, and Romans are all in this book! The city of Rome was founded in 753 BCE, and the Roman Empire lasted over a thousand years. During that time, Rome ruled a good part of Europe, western Asia, and northern Africa.

 A thousand years? That's almost as old as my grandmother.

 Funny, Arlo. According to legend, it all started with two twin boys, Romulus and Remus. They were the sons of Mars, who was the Roman god of war. When they were babies, Romulus and Remus were kidnapped by their evil

uncle. He threw them in the Tiber River to drown. But they didn't! A mother wolf found them and took care of them. Later, a shepherd raised them.

At some point, Mars was reunited with his sons, and he told them to build a city at the spot where they were found. So they built Rome. But sadly, the two brothers fought, and Romulus killed Remus with a rock. Romulus became the first king of Rome.

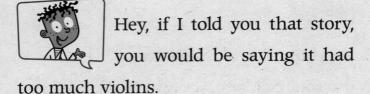 Hey, if I told you that story, you would be saying it had too much violins.

 Not violins, Arlo! Violence!

 I knew that. But it doesn't even matter because it's just another one of those ancient myths, right?

 Right.

 So it never happened?

 Probably not.

 Then why did you tell us all that stuff? This is supposed to be a book of fast *facts*.

 To the Romans, myths were facts. Since they believed Rome was started by the son of a god, they felt it had to be more powerful than any other city.

An Average Day in Ancient Rome

 Let's look at what a typical day was like in Roman times. The first thing you'd do in the morning, of course, would be to turn off your alarm clock . . .

They didn't have alarm clocks in ancient Rome, Arlo! The first thing you'd do would be to get dressed! Most men and women wore a loose linen outfit called a tunic. Roman boys wore a tunic that went down to their knees. It was white, and it had a crimson border. When he became a man, he wore an all-white tunic.

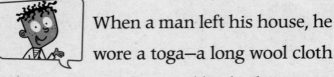 When a man left his house, he wore a toga—a long wool cloth that was wrapped around his body. Roman families would spin their own woolen fabric. If the family was rich, slaves were forced to do the job. Rich families also imported silk from China and cotton from India. That was very expensive.

Statue depicting Roman orator Cicero in his toga

Roman women wore togas too, until the second century BCE, when they weren't allowed to wear them anymore. No fair! Married women wore stolas, which were made of linen. In cold weather, they wore shawls called "pallas" over their stolas.

 Romans wore leather shoes. There were two types. "Calceus" was a sandal with an open toe and foot strap. "Soleae" were regular shoes. Senators and noblemen wore red shoes.

 Women wore pearl necklaces, hairpins, earrings, bracelets,

and rings. They often dyed their hair and wore hairpieces to make their hair look thicker or longer. The men wore rings, sometimes one on each finger. Men and women both used pins called "fibulae" to fasten their clothes together.

 Kids wore lockets around their neck called "bullae." They were given to them when they were born, and they contained an amulet as a protection against evil. A girl would wear her bulla until

Gold bulla, 5th century BCE

the night before her wedding day. A boy would wear his bulla until the day he became a citizen. If a boy grew up to become a successful general, he would wear his bulla in parades.

 Next, it's time to talk about school, Arlo.

 Ugh, no! Not that! Kids had to go to school in Roman times?

 Well, only the boys.

 What?! That's not fair!

 I know, right? Girls should be allowed to go to school too. But you'll love this, Arlo. Not only did the boys have to go to school, but they went to school *seven days a week*! And school started before sunrise and the boys didn't get dismissed until late afternoon.

 No! I would have run away to Antarctica to go live with the penguins.

 It gets worse, Arlo. The Romans believed that a boy would learn better if he was afraid of being beaten. So if a boy did the least little thing wrong, two slaves were made to

hold him down while his tutor beat him
with a leather whip.

 That's awful! I'll never call Ella
Mentry School strict again!

 There were actually two kinds
of schools. Boys who were
twelve and younger learned how to read,
write, and do math. Older boys learned
public speaking. It was really important in
ancient Rome to be a good speaker.

 At least they didn't have to
read books, right? Books are
boring.

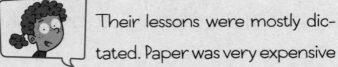 Their lessons were mostly dictated. Paper was very expensive anyway. So students would write on a wax tablet until they proved they could write well. Then they were allowed to use papyrus. The ink was a mixture of gum, soot, and the ink from an octopus. If it was dark, the boys used candles or oil lamps so they could see what they were doing.

We should talk about what the grown-ups of ancient Rome did all day. You couldn't get a job as a video game designer or an Uber driver in those days. But you could be a haruspex.

 What's *that*?

It's a liver reader! You've heard of palm readers, right? In ancient Rome, they would take the liver from a dead animal and "read" it. A person who did that was called a "haruspex." That must have been a weird job!

There were lots of more normal jobs. Most Romans who lived in the countryside were farmers. In the cities, people became soldiers, merchants, lawyers, teachers, tax collectors, and engineers. Craftsmen were needed to make dishes, pots, and jewelry. Actors, musicians, and dancers were needed to entertain people.

Roman Fun

Speaking of entertaining people, the Romans had a lot of fun. Well, at least the boys and men did. They went swimming and had footraces, and wrestling and boxing were really popular. They didn't use boxing gloves. They wrapped their hands in cloth.

Roman boys were expected to be good horseback riders, so they had to learn to do that. Hunting was also popular. They would hunt animals for fun as well as food.

Boys also played ball games like handball, soccer, and field hockey. And finally, they played board games, such as dice ("tes-serae"), knucklebones ("tali" or "tropa"), chess ("latrunculi"), checkers ("calculi"), tic-tac-toe ("terni lapilli"), and backgammon ("tabula").

And do you know what the grown-ups liked to do? The same thing grown-ups like to do now—stand around and talk! The Roman Forum was where all the action was. It was a big open area with a marketplace where business was conducted and festivals took place. Anyone who felt like it could get up and tell the crowd their opinion on any subject. This was called "orating."

Ruins of the Roman Forum in Rome, Italy

 When people force every-body to listen to their opinions today, it's called being obnoxious. The Romans also loved going to the theater.

 They went to movie theaters?

No, there were no movies

back then. But there were lots of plays. People could come see them for free. Once again, women weren't allowed to perform, so female parts were played by men or young boys. No fair!

 The actors often wore masks, and the Romans were famous for pantomime—acting without words. It must have been pretty quiet, so the audience felt free to talk out loud in the middle of the play and discuss it with the people sitting next to them.

 That's rude. And do you know what the audience would do if they didn't like the play? They'd throw

food, sticks, or stones at the actors! Acting was a dangerous job back then. The actors weren't rich celebrities, like today. In ancient Rome, acting was considered just above begging.

But when the Romans wanted *real* excitement, they would go to the Circus Maximus. It wasn't like our circus. Back then, a circus was a big open-air ground used for public events. The Circus Maximus could hold up to 250,000 people, and it was used mostly for chariot racing.

Ruins of the Circus Maximus in Rome, Italy

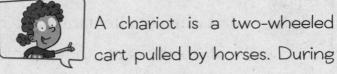 A chariot is a two-wheeled cart pulled by horses. During a race, twelve chariots would circle seven times around the track. There were four teams—blue, green, red, and white. Chariot racing was really popular. Attendance was free to all. On race days, the streets would be just about

Depiction of chariot racing on an ancient Roman coin

deserted because everyone was at the Circus Maximus.

 I bet chariot racing was really dangerous.

 Oh yeah. Accidents happened all the time. Sometimes, the drivers would get trampled to death.

 I don't approve of such violence.

 What do you have against—?

 Arlo!

 If you think chariot racing was dangerous, you probably don't want to hear about what happened in the Colosseum.

 Oh, I've heard of the Colosseum. It was the biggest stadium in Rome and it could seat fifty thousand people. It took twelve years to build.

 Well, Rome wasn't built in a day, you know.

 The Colosseum is still there. You can go there today. For its time, it was amazing. The Colosseum is four stories high, and made from stone and concrete. In just three minutes, all the spectators could get in or out. It even had a cloth sunroof so people could sit in

the shade on a hot day.

So what sorts of events did they have there? Ball games? Dog shows? Art exhibits? Rock concerts? I guess in those days, rock concerts would be concerts with real rocks, huh?

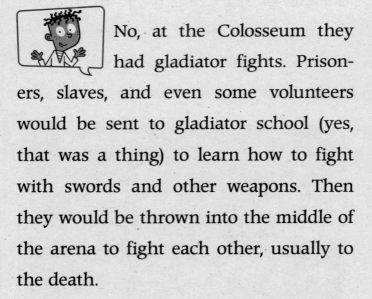 No, at the Colosseum they had gladiator fights. Prisoners, slaves, and even some volunteers would be sent to gladiator school (yes, that was a thing) to learn how to fight with swords and other weapons. Then they would be thrown into the middle of the arena to fight each other, usually to the death.

 To the *death*? And that was considered to be entertain-ment?

When in Rome, do as the Romans do! Sometimes, the gladiators would fight against lions or other animals. In fact, five *thousand* animals were killed on the day the Colosseum opened. History experts think more than a half a million people and over a million animals were killed there.

That is unbelievable!

Well, not all of the fights ended in death. When a gladiator was about to get killed, he might beg for mercy. Sometimes, it would be up to the spectators or the politicians in the crowd to decide if he should live or die.

 Why? Why? Why would they have these horrible shows?

 The emperors put on free gladiator shows because they thought it would make them more popular. If the citizens were distracted and amused by these spectacles, they wouldn't notice how hard their lives were, and they wouldn't rise up and revolt.

 It *all* sounds revolting to me. I'm just glad we don't have anything like that today.

Ever hear of professional wrestling? Mixed martial arts? Boxing?

Go Take a Bath!

 After all that blood and gore and guts, the Romans must have needed to relax. I guess that's why they were seriously into taking baths. Yes, baths! They considered it an important part of a healthy lifestyle.

 Men—once again, no women— would go to the bathhouse to get clean and hang out with friends. The bathhouses had gardens, gyms, and libraries, and they were decorated with statues and mosaics.

When you entered a bathhouse, you would take off your clothes and give them to an attendant. Then you might do some exercises in the gym to work up a sweat. Next, a slave would rub your body with oil and scrape it off. Then you'd hit the baths. First a warm bath (tepidarium), then a hot bath (caldarium), and finally a cold bath (frigidarium). Some bathhouses also had regular swimming pools.

 The Romans really cared about the way they looked.

Ruins of the Baths of Caracalla in Rome, Italy

Rich women would buy sweat and dirt scraped off the skin of famous gladiators. Why? Because they used it as face cream! They also used crushed snails or the milk of a donkey as moisturizer. And that's not all. They would use crushed ant eggs to highlight their eyebrows and smear lead paste on their faces because they wanted to look pale.

I don't know if they had beauty parlors, but women (and men) would dye their hair with oil mixed in earthworm ashes. Yuck! Oh, and men who were going bald would rub on hippopotamus skin.

 The Romans were weird! As long as we're on the subject of baths, we really should mention the ancient Roman toilets.

 I suppose there's no stopping you, Arlo.

 Hey, when you gotta go, you gotta go, right? A public toilet was called a "forica," and it had multiple seats. So you would pee and poop next to a bunch of people at the same time. It must have been like a big party. A pooping party!

With all those people sitting around going to the bathroom at the same time, there could be a buildup of methane gas in the sewer system. Sometimes, it got so bad that the toilet would explode underneath you. Pow! I guess that was how they knew the party was over.

It's times like this when I wish we didn't have to always include facts in these books.

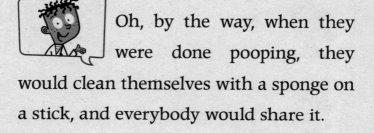 Oh, by the way, when they were done pooping, they would clean themselves with a sponge on a stick, and everybody would share it.

 Okay, I think I'm going to throw up.

 You're gonna like this one, Andrea. Do you know what chariot racers drank for energy?

 Milk? Coffee? Vitamin water?

 Goat poop!

 No!

 It's true. They would boil it in vinegar or grind it into a powder and mix it into drinks for a little late afternoon pick-me-up. And speaking of goat poop, the Roman statesman Cato the Elder said that if a baby couldn't fall asleep, the parents should put some goat dung in the baby's diaper.

 The Romans used diapers?

 What, you thought the babies

would just poop all over the place? That would have been disgusting!

 Can we stop talking about poop now? This is grossing me out.

Okay, let's talk about peeing. In ancient Rome, pee was a big business. They would gather it in public urinals. It was taxed by the government. People made their living going door to door with a big vat to collect pee. They used to sing that song "Urine the Money."

Okay, that last one was a joke.

Very funny, Arlo. What did they do with all that urine?

 You won't believe this. They washed their clothes in it! No kidding! Pee has ammonia in it, so it was good for cleaning. You would take your clothes to a "fullery" where workers would stomp around barefoot in big tubs filled with pee. They were the first washing machines!

 That may be the most disgusting thing I've ever heard.

 Oh yeah? If you think *that's*

disgusting, in some places people used pee as mouthwash! It's true!

 Okay, I've had enough of this.

Roman Technology

 This is going to blow your mind, Andrea. In the year CE 218, Emperor Varius Avitus Bassianus invented the whoopee cushion! It's true! He would blow up animal bladders and slip them on the chairs of his guests so it would make a farting noise when they sat down.

 That's really interesting, Arlo.

 Do you really think so?

No. I just said that so I could change the subject. Let's talk about some *important* Roman innovations. Like arches. The Romans didn't invent the arch, but they used it to build bridges as well as giant public buildings, including the Colosseum.

They also were master road builders. They built nearly fifty-five *thousand* miles of roads and highways. That's how they expanded their empire—they could move soldiers, products, and information over a vast territory. They were also the first to use road signs and mile markers.

Do you know who invented

Roman numerals? The Romans! So they have the perfect name! Roman numerals were invented as a way to count stuff. The only problem was that there was no way to say "zero" with Roman numerals. It's kind of hard to do math if you don't have zeros. I wish we still used Roman numerals today. Because we wouldn't have to do math!

 Do you know what an aqueduct is, Arlo?

 Sure. That's a duck that goes swimming. An aqua duck.

 No! An aqueduct is sort of

like a bridge that carries water from one place to another. The Romans figured out how to move water from rivers and springs to their cities many miles away. Once the water reached the city, they could collect it in reservoirs and use it for their baths, fountains, sewers, and toilets. The most amazing part is that they did this all without pumps, pipes, or machines. They moved water all over the Roman Empire by just using the force of gravity!

Ruins of a Roman aqueduct in Rome, Italy

They also invented central heating. They would warm a room from under the floor. Rich people had running water and central heating in their houses.

The Romans also invented the shopping mall! The first one was built by the emperor Trajan. It had multiple levels and over 150 stores. I love shopping!

In Part 2, we learned that the doctors in ancient Greece had some weird ideas about medical care. Well, wait until our readers hear about the doctors in ancient Rome! They thought the cure for epilepsy was to drink human blood! They thought you could cure a headache by taking an herb growing near the head of a statue and wrapping it around your neck! They thought the way to treat strains and bruises was to rub them with wild boar's poop!

They thought the way to make a pregnant woman give birth was to take a stone that had killed three living creatures and throw it over the roof of the woman's house! They thought that if a woman wanted to have a baby with black eyes, she should eat a shrew, which is a small mole-like animal!

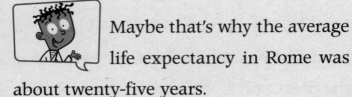 Maybe that's why the average life expectancy in Rome was about twenty-five years.

But that's because of the high rate of infant mortality. They say that as many as half of all the children died before they reached the age of ten.

To be fair, the Romans also invented bronze scalpels, bone drills, forceps, and other tools that their doctors used to save lives. They figured out that dipping medical tools into hot water before surgery would prevent patients from getting infections.

The Romans knew they needed a calendar so everybody in the vast empire would have something to put up on their refrigerators.* So they created a calendar based on the sun, with twelve months in a year. It was called the Julian calendar, in honor of Julius Caesar. The only problem was, the calendar miscalculated the solar year by eleven and a half minutes. Oops! A new and improved calendar was adopted in CE 1582. It was called the Gregorian calendar, named after Pope Gregory XIII.

---

* That's a joke. They didn't have tape or magnets back then, so how could they possibly put anything up on a refrigerator?

Writing used to be on clay tablets and scrolls. The Romans invented the "codex." It was a stack of bound pages—the first books. They also invented the newspaper. It was called "Acta Diurna," or "Daily Events." Handwritten sheets were issued every day and put up in the Roman Forum for citizens to read. The sheets gave news on politics, trials, military campaigns, executions, and scandals.

The Romans also invented concrete! They combined lime, volcanic ash, and water with volcanic rocks to make a substance that was strong and lasted a long time. That's why structures like the Pantheon, the Colosseum, and the Roman Forum are still standing today.

Food, Glorious Food

 Do you know what ancient Romans ate, Arlo?

 Uh, food?

 Right! You're so smart. One popular dish was "pottage," a stew with chopped vegetables, bits of meat, cheese, and herbs.

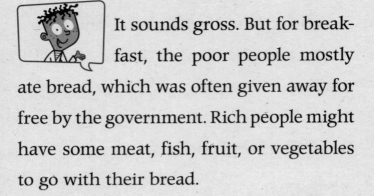 It sounds gross. But for breakfast, the poor people mostly ate bread, which was often given away for free by the government. Rich people might have some meat, fish, fruit, or vegetables to go with their bread.

 I knew that. But did you know that they didn't have sugar? They used honey to sweeten their food.

 I knew that. But did you know they didn't have forks? They did have spoons and knives, though. Slaves were made to cut up the food for rich people.

 A Roman lunch was usually bread, salad, olives, cheese, fruit, nuts, and meat or fish left over from the previous night. After lunch, rich people would take a two-hour break called a "sexta hora."

They ate slushies made from snow brought down from the mountains. For dinner, they would eat exotic foods like stork, roast parrot, flamingo, peacock tongues, and dormice.

 Dormice? Do you mean dormice as in *mice* mice? They ate mice? Ugh, gross!

You think *that's* gross? One

popular dish was a chicken stuffed inside a duck, the duck stuffed inside a goose, the goose stuffed inside a pig, and the pig stuffed inside a cow! They would cook that whole thing and eat so much that they'd throw up into bowls that were kept around the table. Then, after that, they'd go back and eat some more!

 It would have been a lot easier if they just invented the peanut butter and jelly sandwich.

What Did Ancient Romans Believe?

 Like the Egyptians and the Greeks, the Romans believed

in *lots* of gods. I mean *tons*! There was a god of trees. Rocks had a god. Different parts of a house each had their own god. They even had a god for doors (Forculus) and a god for hinges (Cardea).

 Hinges? Hinges need a god?

 Yeah, and so did door*ways*. The god Janus protected doorways and gates to keep homes and buildings safe from evil spirits. The Romans needed so many gods that they took some from the Greeks and changed their names.

The gods supposedly watched over the people. Whenever something bad happened to somebody, it meant they hadn't worshipped the gods correctly. That's why every city built temples to the gods, and citizens would visit the temple every day with offerings and sacrifices.

 Do you want to know my favorite Roman gods?

 I'm almost afraid to hear them.

 Cloacina was the goddess of sewers. Sterquilinus was the god of poop. That's right! They had a god of poop! Isn't that hilarious?

 Arlo, you made those gods up!

 I did not! Look it up in your encyclopedia if you don't believe me.

Wow, you're right! But let's focus on the more famous gods and goddesses. Like Jupiter. He was the most powerful god, and king of all the gods. When he got mad, he would hurl a thunderbolt. Juno was Jupiter's wife, and also his sister. That must have been weird. She watched over the women of Rome.

Neptune was Jupiter's brother, and the lord of the sea. His other brother, Pluto, was the lord of the underworld.*

---

* Lord of the underwear?

Jupiter had sons—Mars, Mercury, and Apollo. Mars was
the god of war. He was mean, and nobody

liked him. Mercury was the messenger of the gods, so he was sort of like a mail carrier. He knew everything about everybody. Apollo was the god of the sun, light, and music.

There were lots of goddesses too. Diana was the goddess of the hunt. Minerva was the goddess of wisdom. Vesta was the goddess of hearth and home. And of course, Venus was the goddess of love and beauty.

 Yuck! Gross! You said the L word!

 Oh, you'll like *this*, Arlo.

Venus's son was named Cupid. He carried a bow and arrow with him. If Cupid hit you with one of his arrows, you fell in love with the very next person you saw. Isn't that romantic?

 To get hit by an arrow? I don't *think* so!

The Romans had all kinds of other weird characters that they believed in. Orpheus was a famous musician. When he played his lyre, it would cast spells and soothe a savage beast. Vulcan made the first woman out of clay. Hercules was half man, half god, and very strong. Pegasus was a winged horse that could fly. Cerberus was the three-headed dog that guarded the entrance to the underworld.

 The Romans were weird.

Military

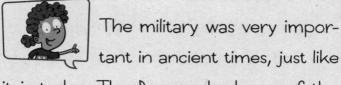 The military was very important in ancient times, just like it is today. The Romans had one of the most powerful armies of any empire.

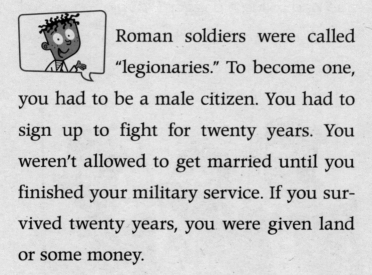 Roman soldiers were called "legionaries." To become one, you had to be a male citizen. You had to sign up to fight for twenty years. You weren't allowed to get married until you finished your military service. If you survived twenty years, you were given land or some money.

 It wasn't easy to survive. You

had to march as much as twenty-one miles in five hours. If that doesn't sound so hard, consider this—the whole time, you had to wear an iron helmet, armor made from strips of iron, and you had to carry a tall shield. Not only that, but you also had to lug a dagger ("pugio"), a sword ("gladius"), a spear ("hasta"), and a bow and arrow.

The Roman army was *huge*. One legion included over five thousand soldiers. A legion was divided up into a smaller group called a "cohort," and the cohort was divided into groups of eighty men called "centuries." The leaders of each century were called "centurions," so they had the perfect name.

Of course, the leader of *all* those soldiers was the emperor. The word "emperor" comes from the Latin "imperator," which means "military commander." Do you know how you could tell somebody was an emperor or senator in ancient Rome?

 They drove a Ferrari?

No, dumbhead! There were no cars in those days! You could tell somebody was an emperor or senator because their clothing was purple!

That was my next guess. Let's talk about some of the most famous Roman emperors.

Julius Caesar never had the *title* of emperor, but he was a powerful general who took control of the Roman Empire from the Senate. In 44

BCE, he was named "Dictator Perpetuus," or dictator for life. Unfortunately, his life didn't last very long, because the same year he was assassinated by members of the Senate. They didn't think one person should control the whole empire.

By the way, when Julius Caesar died, he left money to every citizen of Rome.

In today's dollars, it would be about $270 per person.

 Augustus was Julius Caesar's son, and he was the first real emperor. In forty years, he built more roads, started the postal service, improved the police and fire departments, and nearly doubled the size of the empire.

Roman statue of Augustus Caesar

Caligula was not a nice guy. He killed people who he didn't

like, and demanded to be worshipped like a god. In the end, he was assassinated by his bodyguards.

By the way, it wasn't unusual for Roman emperors to get murdered by their enemies, usually with poison. So do you know what some of the emperors did to prevent that from happening? Every day, they would drink or eat a little bit of poison. They thought that would help them build up an immunity to it.

One more thing about Caligula—he really liked horses. In fact, he tried to make his favorite horse—Incitatus—a consul, which was the most important job in the government.

Claudius's family didn't want him to be emperor. But when Caligula was assassinated, there were no other choices, so Claudius became emperor for thirteen years. He wasn't a bad one either. He passed good laws and started many building projects. While he was in charge, the Romans conquered Britain.

Nero was no sweetheart. At first, the people liked him because he would go chariot racing, sing songs, and recite poetry in public. But at some point, he went crazy. He started executing his enemies, or people he thought were enemies. He had his mother killed, and it was rumored that he murdered his wife. Ultimately, Nero was tried and sentenced to death, though he took his own life before he was executed, bringing a sad end to a sad tale.

 Hadrian traveled all across the Roman Empire. He realized it was too big to defend, so he had his armies withdraw to borders that could be protected more easily. He also built a stone border wall that stretched seventy-three miles across Britain. It was called Hadrian's Wall, and parts of it are still there today.

Hadrian's Wall in Northumberland National Park

After five hundred years of ruling a huge part of the world, the Roman Empire collapsed. Why? There were a lot of reasons. Some of the emperors were nuts, of course. There were constant struggles for power, and a lot of corruption. The Roman Empire was too big to control. There were financial problems because so much money was spent fighting wars. Christianity was on the rise. And the Romans faced powerful enemies, including Germanic tribes like the Goths and the Vandals. That's where we get the word "vandal"—people who destroy stuff.

Historians usually say CE 476 was the

year the Roman Empire ended. The last of the emperors was Romulus, which I guess makes sense. After all, it was a little boy named Romulus and his twin brother who created Rome in the first place.

Or so the legend goes, anyway.

More Weird Fast Facts about Ancient Rome . . .

You wouldn't want to be left-handed in ancient Rome. Lefties were considered unlucky and evil. In fact, the word "sinister" comes from the Latin word "sinistra," which means "left." You know the expression "getting up on the wrong side of the bed"? Supposedly, Romans got up on the "right side" because the left side was evil.

It was hard to be a woman in the early days of ancient Rome. A woman's job was to take care of her home and teach younger women how to cook, sew, and run a household. They couldn't own property, inherit, sign a contract, work outside the home, or run a business. They couldn't defend themselves in court. No fair!

Women had to be under the control of a male guardian all the time. That might mean her father, her husband, or even her oldest male child.

 So a son could boss around his own mom?

That's right. Later, when Rome became an empire, things began to change and women got more rights. But they still couldn't vote or hold office.

We've mentioned slaves a few times here. It sounds awful to us today, but slavery was an accepted practice to the Romans. One out of every four people was a slave. A rich man might own five hundred slaves. An emperor might have twenty *thousand*.

If someone was captured in battle, he might be sent back to Rome to be a slave. Abandoned children might end up as slaves. If a slave had a baby, the baby was automatically a slave. Sometimes, a father would sell an older child into slavery. Every so often, a slave would save up money and buy his or her freedom. But unfortunately, most slaves were slaves for life.

What did the wealthy Romans force their slaves to do? Lots of stuff. Slaves were made to help dress their master, walk his kids to school, clean the house, wash the clothes, prepare

174

meals, and serve food to guests. If a guest had to go home after dark, a slave might escort them with a lighted torch.

 Probably the only time of year that slaves were happy was Saturnalia. That was a festival in which slaves and masters would switch places.

Monte Testaccio in Rome is probably the most valuable garbage dump in the world. Archaeologists found fifty-three *million* ceramic vases there. I guess they didn't have recycling back then.

 The month of January was named after Janus, the Roman god of beginnings. He had two faces. One looked back to the last year and the other looked forward to the new year. The month of April comes from the

Latin word "aperire," which means "to open"—like when a flower opens. The month of August was named after Emperor Augustus.

Funerals have always been expensive. In ancient Rome, people who didn't have much money would join burial clubs. Money would be taken out of their salary to help pay for their future funeral. And by the way, our word "funeral" comes from "funus," which means "torch" in Latin. They believed a flaming torch would guide dead people into the afterlife and scare away evil spirits.*

---

* The Romans had beautiful cemeteries. People were dying to get in.

The Twelve Tables were important laws of the Romans, which they carved into tablets. Some of them were weird. Like, it was against the law to write a song that insulted somebody else. Another one of the Twelve Tables said it was perfectly legal to pick up fruit that had fallen on someone else's farm.

The Romans had a weird system for choosing the best puppy out of a litter. Get this—they'd soak a long string in oil and make it into a big circle. Then they'd put all the puppies in the middle of the circle and set the string on fire. The mother dog, of course, would freak out. She would jump into the middle to rescue the puppies one at a time. The order that she rescued the puppies indicated which puppies were the best and which were the worst. What I want to know is how they got the puppies to stay inside the circle.

Clowns were really popular in Roman times. They even had different kinds of clowns. A "sannio" was a mime. A "stupidus" (yes, that's where the word "stupid" comes from) was a fool who was bald or wore a long pointed hat and a multicolored outfit. He made fun of the serious actors and was famous for making riddles and having slapstick fights.

 The first mooning in history took place in Roman times! What happened was that some Roman soldiers were sent to keep an eye on some citizens in case they revolted. A priest named Flavius Josephus wrote a description of what happened. He said one soldier lifted "up the back of his garments, turned his face away, and with his bottom to them, crouched in a shameless way and released at them a foul-smelling sound where they were offering sacrifice."

That brave soldier threw the first moon, and the rest is ancient history!

Well, Arlo, it looks like you've managed to ruin another

perfectly interesting subject by talking about pooping and peeing and mooning and other gross, disgusting things. I hope you're proud of yourself.

 I am!

The Ending

 Congratulations, My Weird School readers! Now you know *all* there is to know about ancient Egypt, Greece, and Rome.

 They do *not*, Arlo.

 Well, that's true. I could say a

bunch more about other gross stuff that people did in ancient times. Would you like to hear it?

 No!

 It's just as well. I have more important things to do. Like go take out the garbage.

 And I have to go reread my encyclopedia. But there's lots more cool stuff to know about ancient history. So poke around. Go online. Go to the library and look for other books on these subjects.

 Ugh, disgusting! You used the L word and the B word in the same sentence!

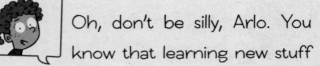 Oh, don't be silly, Arlo. You know that learning new stuff is cool. It's fun to impress grown-ups with how smart you are. They think kids are a bunch of dumbheads who don't know anything. But we'll show *them*, right?

Right! Maybe you readers will be able to convince your parents that the ancient Egyptians invented toothpaste. Maybe you'll be able to convince your teacher that the ancient Greek

doctors would eat a piece of earwax to figure out why a patient wasn't feeling well.
Maybe you'll be able to convince your
librarian that the ancient Romans would
cook a chicken stuffed inside a duck,
which was stuffed inside a goose, which
was stuffed inside a pig, which was stuffed
inside a cow.

But it won't be easy!*

---

* Ha-ha, made you look! Hey, the book is finished.
Why are you still hanging around?

I Like WEIRD Books.

My Weird School

Discover more in the My Weird School series from Dan Gutman

My Weirder School

My Weirdest School

My Weirder-est School

My Weird School Fast Facts

My Weird School Daze

My Weird Tips

HARPER
An Imprint of HarperCollinsPublishers

www.harpercollinschildrens.com